BAKE MY BRAIN

by

HUME CRONYN

Mosaic Press
Oakville-New York-London

Canadian Cataloguing in Publication Data

Cronyn, Hume, 1957-
  Bake my brain
Poems.

ISBN 0-88962-543-3

I.Title.

PS8555.R65B3 1993   C811'.54
PR9199.3.C76B3 1993

Published by MOSAIC PRESS, P.O. Box 1032, Oakville, Ontario, L6J 5E9, Canada. Offices and warehouse at 1252 Speers Road, Units #1&2, Oakville, Ontario L6L 5N9, Canada.

Mosaic Press acknowledges the assistance of the Canada Council and the Ontario Arts Council in support of its publishing programme.

Copyright © Hume Cronyn, 1993
Design by Susie Parker
Cover collage by Eric Meissner
Typeset by Jackie Ernst

Printed and bound in Canada.

ISBN 0-88962-543-3 PB

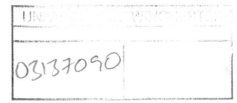

MOSAIC PRESS:
In Canada:
    MOSAIC PRESS, 1252 Speers Road, Units 1&2, Oakville, Ontario L6L 5N9, Canada. P.O. Box 1032, Oakville, Ontario L6J 5E9

In the United States:
    Distributed to the trade in the United States by: National Book Network, Inc., 4720-A Boston Way, Lanham, MD 20706, USA

In the U.K.:
    John Calder (Publishers) Ltd., 9-15 Neal Street, London, WCZH 9TU, England.

CONTENTS

I

II

III

IV

V

I

I WANT TO BAKE MY BRAIN IN A BIRTHDAY CAKE

I

I want to be angry.

I want to burn my soggy flesh,
Tear out my mushy bones,
Find one inch of steel.

I want to cut off my ear,
Cut off one of my testicles,
Change my name to One.

I want to tear off my skin, use it as a door mat;
Pull out my hair, use it as a scouring pad;
Cut off my thumbs, plant them in the garden.

I want to cut off my shadow, soak it in milk;
Rip out my throat, wash it in bowls of music;
Tear out my brain, bake it in a birthday cake.

II

I want newspapers to publish front-page news PROMETHEUS BOUND and THE BOOK OF JOB.

I want Russia and America to exchange governments for at least five years.

I want all walls to break into flowers, all roofs to be sky, and the stars to bend down and illuminate the pages of late-night readers.

I want massive theatres to be constructed in every city. I want Periclean Athens and Renaissance Rome to be staged daily, the Golden Ages emulated. I want Buchenwald and Hiroshima to be staged daily, the horrors purged forever.

I want people to notice all the dedicated lovers, to erase Hollywood from their minds.
I want Albert Camus who said, 'There are only three great loves in a century', to rise up from his grave and confess his error.

I want John Lennon to fall down, and stand up again. I want all guns to be loaded with feathers, and all people who pull the trigger to be less than feathers blown away in the grey dust.

I want many mothers and fathers. I'm sick of the man who makes it on his own. I want my debts to be enormous.

I want all cars to break out in sores, gas tanks to spill over with sperm, tires to turn into rivers of licorice, and all cars to float off and hurtle over the nearest cliff.
And all those people who wish to share the destiny of their cars, to do so.

I want people to wander the earth, use their legs once again, let their lungs fill up with enough air to fly a kite, let their heads be flushed out with mountain streams, their eyes to light up with birthday candles, their hearts to glitter with a Christmas tree.

I want all old people to rebel against their dogfood dinners, smash their TVs, burn their historical romances. I want them to gorge on steak and pastries, seek out new sons and daughters, rediscover love in parks and railway stations.

I want all politicians, all corporate bosses, all union officials, all military commanders to turn into leaves, and learn about photosynthesis.

I want all people to change race several times in a lifetime, change occupations, countries, languages, religions.

I want all people who are gutted by hatred, doubt, and cynicism to sit in their bathtub and sing Bach's 'Mass in B Minor,' Beethoven's 'Missa Solemnis.'

I want turtles to wander the city streets in rush hour, pigeons to roost in safety deposit boxes, mating deer to travel the underground.

I want all clocks to throw up their hands and stop ticking. I want them to shine like the sun, and all people who work to the clock to throw down their pencils, pens, typewriters, shovels, assembly lines, profit and loss statements, and revel in the sun.

I want a child for every year that I am over thirty.

I want to watch the life of legs from underneath tables, talk to cats in nursery rhymes, make snowmen like the angel Gabriel, dunk for apples in tubs full of water.

I want to give my children portions of my heart, portions of my mind, portions of my imagination. I want to build them houses in the trees, and provide them with root ladders.

More than anything, I want man to mend the shattered black-jug earth so that it can once again hold the sacred milk that God pours into it, and that man can once again drink from it.

BLUE BEGONIAS

I'm listening to a friend's short story
- Titled 'Blue Begonias' -
And I think of you, untitled,
Who irons your red T-shirt on the floor,
Who wears purple and red when days are grey,
Who has a breakfast of cappuccino
And licks a fingertip sparkling with white sugar.

'Love is like a conjurer's room full of dead white rabbits.'

Love fits in no room!
It wears two holes in the sleeve of a sweater,
Earrings that dangle like clock chimes,
More alive than a hundred hours in a day,
Dark as the glass of water you hold.
What birds you weave on your Navaho loom!
What stairways you build -
Deeper than any burrowed hole,
Higher than the miles of apples you eat.

*'Like falling naked into a colliseum of red hot nails, and still I felt
ecstasy.'*

Sometimes you spell your name with C, sometimes with K.
Will I ever be able to pronounce it?
Will I ever speak German?
You only sleep with me half the night:
You bite my knuckles, leave your teeth marks,
And when I kiss your underarms
- No colliseums of prickly deodorant -
I feel ecstacy.

'Is an inventory any way to start a love affair? I want improvisation.'

Yes to both!
You wear two red elastics in your hair,
Work two days a week at British Rail,
James Joyce hangs above your bed,
There is a window in the knee of your jeans.

How good you look in my tweed coat,
Too big for me, huge on you,
The pockets full of candy wrappers -
Though you swear you could live on bread alone.
Thank God you are no Gretchen,
You are a master of improvisation:
You snuff out your cigarettes in my lemon halves;
Oh for those days when you claim you could never be a star pilot,
Because when you broke the sound barrier, all your fillings would fly out.
I love you like the sun,
You pull blue begonias from my teeth.

DREAM ROOM

I dream of a ladder in my head.
I climb to the top, come to a trapdoor.

At first it refuses to budge, then it swings open.
I enter into a room with shining windows.

The walls are white. They turn red,
Then yellow, then waver with morning glories.

A bare lightbulb hangs from a cord, turns
Into a skull, a foetal child, the aroma of pears.

A tiger crouched in the corner leaps at me,
Turns into a bird that sits on my shoulder.

In the middle of the room, an apple lies on the floor,
It turns into an apple tree, spring, summer.

A girl sits on the bed, laughing,
She turns into a window, a candle.

Night plunges into the room:
A shark fin, scent of oranges, daylight.

I begin to sing: moons float from my mouth,
Fish swim through my veins.

I feel at home in this room,
I turn into an owl, a birthday cake, a room.

WARDROBE UPBRINGING

I was a hanger-kid once:
They zipped me up in a heavy coat
And hung me in the hall wardrobe -
My feet, several inches from the ground.

At first the door was left open:
I saw the sun through the window,
The walls bright with stripes,
The beachball deflated in the corner,
The telephone polished and always busy,
The carpets worn by successive hoovers,
The doormat hanging on the clothesline,
The shadows swept down the cellar stairs.

Slowly, the door began to close.
Inch by inch, it closed on me.
I put on weight, especially around the waist:
The coat rack sagged, my feet touched the ground.
It was bright with fluorescent light,
My eyes grew puffy from the heat;
It was crowded with stiff black coats
And bulging furs, and the smell of moth balls.

Once they came to comfort me,
'Life's like that,' they said,
'It shrinks with age
- Children, job, responsibilities -
But at least your feet are on the ground.'

'No,' I said, 'it was all wrong from the beginning!'
I tore myself from the hanger, threw off my coat;
I smashed the window, the sun felt good on my forehead;
I buried the telephone in the garden, visited friends;
I threw out the hoover, let the shadows drift upstairs;
I stripped the walls, painted them with clowns and acrobats;
I put out the doormat, everyone came for breakfast:
We played with the beachball, it sprung from fingertips to fingertips.

THE DAY HAS DIRTY HAIR

Like tapeworms we travel up intestines of chrome
That starve us with shocks of light
And advertisements of vodka and stockings.
Sleep is still in our mouths,
The day locked in briefcases.

Discharged from Holborn station,
We watch clouds wander like wrapped-up minds
Who have forgotten their home addresses
And travel from door to door
Trying to peddle encyclopedias and hoovers
In exchange for a warm shirt and an idea.
We do not notice our bric-a-brac coats
(held together by animal horns and saliva);
We do not notice our dyed and curled skin.
We trot out our hopes like a family of ducklings
To a pond full of church bells and coins.

The day smells like dirty hair,
I am trapped in its greasy growth.
I scratch at the scalp of days,
Dig up flakes of routine hours.
Eyes are grey with profit and loss sheets;
Mouths sticky with stale chocolates;
Noses plugged with bargain prices;
And minds dried like raisins
Are packed in boxes of assorted fruit -
To be snatched at by bank managers,
And tireless purveyors of fancy goods.

I want man to reform the day,
Bring the circus to town.

Bring on the clown,
The day as bright as his nose.

Bring on the acrobat,
The day limber as his cartwheels.

Bring on the midget,
The day populated by smaller ambitions.

Bring on the Cyclops,
The day inspired by third-eye politics.

Bring on the Siamese twins,
The day stripped of separateness.

Bring on the trapeze artist,
The day full of somersaults.

Bring on the hairless freak,
The day bald of pretensions and preening.

Bring on the hunchback,
The day transfigured by Esmeralda.

Bring on the two-headed man,
The day full of ideas.

NICKELODEON

Mother was quiet. I did not speak.
For the first time that rainless summer,
The convertible roof shut out sun and sky.
We were passing through the small town of Aylmer
- On our way to Grandad's Chatham farm -
When a pistol shot in the rear made us jump.
Mother veered into the curb; a flat tire.
The road stretched before us blue in the heat -
Ten miles from Grandad's, wider than an ocean.
Across the street was THE TOWN AND COUNTRY.
I asked Mother, 'How could it be both?'
She said, 'I hope it has a telephone.'

Inside a man wiped down the soda counter,
Talked about the death of J.F.K.
A lady sat bulging in red satin.
She turned on her stool, looked so sad.
Mother and I sat in a red leather booth;
A nickelodeon was mounted on the wall.
I pushed the buttons, flipped the metal rods -
Was surprised when pages turned behind the glass.
I asked mother what it was.

Mother took a nickel from her purse.
I saw a buffalo disappear into the slot.
Music swooped into that sultry room
Like Mother's car swooped when the roof was down.
The lady at the counter sang to the nickel's song.
Mother and I talked for the first time that day,
Talked about last summer on Grandad's farm:
Waking to the song of birds; the robin we nursed;
The pony that nibbled sugar from our hands;
The litter of kittens born in the barn;
Grandad chasing me up and down the garden,
His false teeth clicking in his hand.
The music stopped. A man in black overalls
Entered, shouted, 'Who called about the flat?'
Mother pulled me to her, tears in her eyes,
'Hume, your Grandad is dying.'

11

For weeks I hunted for the perfect nickel -
The buffalo raised and clean in outline,
The faces unsmudged by greasy fingerprints,
The milling fresh from the mint and free from grime.
One day a letter arrived with my name on it:
It was from Grandad, and inside was a nickel.
He said he was thinking of me, and best of luck.
I wrapped the nickel in yellow tissue paper,
Kept it in my trouser's button pocket -
Never mixing it with my other coins.
And each night I unwrapped my nickel,
And dreamt that buffalo roamed my room.

That Sunday the family gathered for dinner.
Grandad was missing, his rocking chair empty
(He rocked his food into his stomach, he said.)
Nine of us ate with bent heads.
Knives and forks clinked on plates.
No one used the salt and pepper;
No one asked for second helpings.
I stood up on my red leather chair,
Unwrapped my coin, and swallowed it,
Sobbing, 'Mother, will I sing?'

SENTENCES

Whenever I want to choke on strawberries and cream,
I hang a sentence around my neck.

Whenever I want to chase a bird gliding on the wind,
I take a sentence for a walk, and stand helpless as it pisses at
    every lamppost.

Whenever I want to sleep a dreamless night,
I go to bed on a sentence.

Whenever I want to cheat my best friend,
I pay with a sentence.

Whenever I want to smash eardrums and crack wineglasses,
I sing the sentences of Proust and Henry James.

Whenever I want to love cheaply,
I kiss with a sentence.

Whenever I want to take a bath and remain dirty,
I scrub myself with a sentence.

Whenever I want to smoke myself out of my room,
I burn a book of sentences.

Whenever I want to hide from myself,
I write in sentences.

THE DISCARDED GLOVE

I hurried after her.
The streets were paved with metal.

Buildings towered, shone like coal.
My mouth was full of stones.

Bulldozers dug up the sidewalk.
I shouted. She turned around.

Her face shone with broken glass.
She held a porcupine,

Stood in a circle of blue light.
The wind lashed us with salt.

She asked if I had broken the hands,
I worried too much about time.

She didn't blame me for the broken glass,
But ambition has a sharp edge.

I said I had broken the minute hand,
But I was having trouble with the other.

Several times I stroked the porcupine.
'Take off your glove,' she said.

I peeled off my glove,
Threw it against a shop window.

I pulled a piece of glass from her cheek.
There was blood. I kissed it.

I wanted to heal the scars.
The hour hand broke, fell from the building.

TO APOLLINAIRE

I never go anywhere
Because there is nowhere to go.
There is nowhere to go
Because I never go anywhere.
The sky shuts me in no matter what the day is -
Either it is cloudy with the mushroom of Hiroshima,
Or it is the savage blue of the airless church.
The evening brings no relief.
The stars are nailed to their crosses,
And, night after night,
A dry bone or two drops from the sky -
Bodies too long on their crosses.
For two thousand years,
Man has nailed himself to the stars,
And dreamt of new wars and new churches
To humble life with one plan,
One God, one country, one father,
One earth, one moon, one sun,
While angry poets starve themselves -
Hunger, the only mind they know;
Hunger, their feeble protest against fat-gutted rulers.
What does it matter?
Apollinaire's long dead and gone.

The maitre d' keeps *carbonnade* of beef in his hat.
He hasn't served a meal in sixty years
Because Apollinaire no longer eats there:
Apollinaire who would eat yet another meal,
His third or fourth, if a friend came by
Late and effusive, or late and distraught.
And over *boeuf en daube* and mounds of spaghetti,
Apollinaire watched his friend mash his food
Into desert flatness with the back of his spoon.
Three times Apollinaire waved his knife:
Three times it cut through the flame of the candle.
'The flame is an upside-down heart,' he said,
'If you starve the candle, you starve the flame.
Paris is a fruit of candlelight:
Acrobats wear the history of the world in their beards;

Around the head of Hugo's statue, the one-winged pihis flies;
The Eiffel Tower shepherds a flock of bleating bridges;
And when the chef at LE CIEL plucks a goose, it snows.
The streets are my bride, how foolish it is to hang yourself from a
    senseless star.
Paris is laden with grapes, and needs the sturdy press of your throat.'
And from each of the nine doors,
Acrobats in yellow leotards streamed in,
Danced around the tables,
Twirled barbells with suns at each end,
And shook red feathers hanging from their hair.
Swallows flew about, and perched on shoulders.
Stars shone from the ripe blue of the ceiling.
Apollinaire's friend swallowed one and said,
'Every man is a God and a father.
I have met my double and he is not death.
Everywhere I shall meet my double now.'
And hungry, he twirled up his spaghetti,
And gulped down his *boeuf en daube*
Till his plate shone, a white moon licked clean.
But Apollinaire died,
Sixty years ago.
Nowhere to go now.
What does it matter?
Apollinaire's long dead and gone.

So I journeyed to the desert,
Dreamt of finding the scented ring of red cedars
That closed around the perfect circle of the lake.
I dreamt that the sky filled with flowers
- I was wrapped in a soft glow of pollen -
A flash of lightning pierced the lake,
And lilies sprang up across the water.
But as I crossed the desert, the road cracked,
And lifting, it rolled up on me.
And I who was walking the white line
Was rolled up in a snail's shell.
My dreamt-of lake turned to salt;
My red cedars turned to blood-thin crosses.
What does it matter?
Apollinaire's long dead and gone.

Then I heard another voice
- A truer voice -
'Apollinaire, I honour you.
You swallowed life like wine,
But with your death, all throats grew dry,
All roads were rerouted to the desert.
I wanted to tread your road
- Drink the wine of cities -
But my road is the skull road.
I am trapped in a snail's shell;
I drink water and snatch at Hamlet's flies;
I live in a hungry decade.
To achieve your way without falseness,
I must cross the desert first...
But I will never lose sight of you Apollinaire.
One day I will break out of my shell,
Then I will follow your road through ripe cities.
What does it matter?
It matters! He sang of life.
Apollinaire's long dead and gone,
But what he sang of never dies.'

II

PALESTROM NAMES HIMSELF

No Name read the German poet Christian Morgenstern
Who invented the immortal character Palmstrom.

Throughout the entire cycle of poems,
No Name misread the name as Palestrom.

He was so taken by the gifts of this character -
By his innumerable magical inventions,

And the anarchy of his quirky mind -
That he decided to take on his name:

Not the name that Morgenstern gave him,
But the name as he misread it.

Palestrom then decided to give his name a philological root.
However, the only language that he knew was English,

So instead of spending years learning languages,
He invented a lost and ancient language.

The first word was 'strom,' meaning man.
PALEMAN. Palestrom liked that.

And that was the end of his invented language -
One word, that was all he needed.

PALEMAN! Somehow, that said a lot about Palestrom.

PALESTROM WANTS TO BE A TOILET

In a previous document, Palestrom revealed
The philological root of his name: PALEMAN.

Now he is having second thoughts about his name.
As much as he likes it,

There is one serious drawback to it:
People will think he is anaemic.

The fact is: he is not anaemic.
Only spiritually so.

He is constantly unsettled by the feeling
That he's the white walls of a lavatory -

Always seeing man reveal himself,
And the more that he sees,

The more he hates his role as a pale spectator.
He longs to play an active part.

He longs to be a toilet.
Not the cold aloofness of walls,

But the still water disturbed,
The act of flushing,

The deep embrace,
The return to still water.

Then Palestrom would no longer be PALEMAN,
He would take on the unadorned name of MAN.

PALESTROM UNLOVED

Palestrom always dresses in brown -
Boring, boring brown! Why not blue or red?

He always dresses in brown -
Shades of earth brown, shades of nondescript.

Today he feels a little uncomfortable:
He's wearing a new shade of brown

- He feels like a chocolate bar -
But still he will visit his girlfriend,

Sport his adventure into a new shade.
However, she fails to notice the change;

In fact, she fails to notice Palestrom at all.
Oh, why doesn't she have a sweet tooth?

PALESTROM TRAINS HIS BODY TO BREAK OUT IN THORNS

Palestrom hates louring after women,
Turning his head this way and that.
He hates lurking after them,
Hates the desire that persists into sleep.

Palestrom thinks it must be hard to be a woman.
How uncomfortable to be always stared at:
Must be like flies lighting on the face.
Palestrom hates causing so much discomfort.

So Palestrom, whenever he becomes desirous,
Has trained his body to break out in thorns.
And in the far corner of his garden,
He grows like the branch of a rose bush.

He grows, and grows, and grows,
Until towering, he reaches the clouds,
And the clouds wrap around him
And caress his thorns until they are worn smooth.

And smoothed, he turns into a rose.
Then, how often he is picked by some woman -
To be worn in her hair, or placed in her bedroom,
Or planted in the warmth of her heart.

PALESTROM REVERSES THE FALL OF THE RAIN

Palestrom loves the rain.
With the first drop knocking on his window
He throws on his long winter coat
And takes to the streets.

He thinks clouds are wandering eyes:
Eyes that see so much of suffering life
That they well up with tears,
And cry, and cry, and cry.

Palestrom loves the rain.
It's a strange sort of comfort to know
He's not the only one who cries for man:
World and he are finally at one.

But sometimes he wonders if he likes the rain
Because so many others run to avoid it.
He likes the sense of weathering it alone,
And facing the world with wide-open eyes.

But recently it has rained so much
He feels that he is indulging himself -
And like the water streaming into the sewers,
He is letting himself be sucked away.

Once in a while it is proper to be sad,
But other times one must fight against it.
So Palestrom decided to reverse the rain.
He closed his eyes and ate an orange,

And with a great force of concentration,
He recomposed the orange in his stomach.
It lay there full and orange;
It lay there warm, and like a child.

And he thought upon this inward sun.
He thought and thought,
Until suddenly, the rain...
It was flung back into the clouds.

PALESTROM FEELS GOOD

Palestrom feels great today
- The skies are blue and warm -
He skips through the streets.
No more winter coats!

No more bulky sweaters!
God, he feels transparent.
What does it matter?
Fish swim through his veins!

Usually they sleep in his feet:
They lie like icicles, so cold,
That Palestrom finds it necessary
To wear three pairs of socks.

But today they surge through his body,
Flick the warmth of fin and tail -
Whoosh, they fly and fling the spray.
God, does Palestrom feel good!

But Palestrom must go to the library:
He's a great believer in discipline.
No matter what the weather is,
He must do a few hours work.

Damn his luck, Ol' Sourpuss sits beside him
- He has never said a word to Palestrom -
But today he also has fish in his blood.
He leans across and whispers to Palestrom,

'This weather sure gives everyone a good flip.'
And Palestrom sees all of London
With fish flipping through their veins.
How wonderful, thinks Palestrom,

Fish even live in this dead place.
But outside! It must be a teeming sea by now.
And Palestrom thanks Ol' Sourpuss,
And strolls out of the library.

PALESTROM PLAYS AT HOUSE

Palestrom's girlfriend is away,
He plays at house.

The plates stack up in columns,
He hangs feathers from the ceiling.

He waters the flowers with milk,
Keeps angelfish in the blender.

He floats red balloons through the rooms,
Spins spider webs from balls of wool.

Carrots rot in the candlesticks,
Birds roost in the fridge.

He plants forget-me-nots in her shoes,
Covers the staircase with tin foil.

He toasts marshmallows for breakfast,
Washes his clothes in her perfume.

He buries the alarm clock in pancake batter,
Grows dandelions in their bed.

He paints measles on the bathroom mirror,
Wraps his sandwiches in her stockings.

He paints the walls with her make-up,
Dresses all the chairs in her blouses.

PALESTROM LOVED

Whenever Palestrom wakes up from a bad night's sleep,
He finds his body covered with creases.

There are two solutions: immersion in a cold bath -
To shock the skin from its wrinkled sleepiness;

Or the measured application of a steaming iron -
To press the skin into tablecloth smoothness.

Palestrom rejects the cold bath:
It reminds him of Christian saints.

Palestrom rejects the steaming iron:
It reminds him of domestic tidiness.

Therefore, there must be a third choice.
There is! Palestrom has a girlfriend:

The warm touch of her lips
Draws out the creases of night.

PALESTROM PICKING

Palestrom is sick of picking his scalp.
He picks his nose all too often.
He is sick of picking his ears and sleepy eyes,
Sick of picking scabs on his chest and back.

Palestrom decides to save everything he picks.
In quart bottles he stores it all:
Dandruff, snot, earwax, and scabs.
In a year he fills four bottles.

Growing old is picking, thinks Palestrom:
When he's forty, it will be five bottles;
When he's fifty, maybe six;
When he's sixty, what will be left?

Palestrom hates the idea of old age,
Hates the idea of what will be left.
One picks, and picks, and picks:
It's not like picking apples.

PALESTROM IS A DREAM OF NOISE

Palestrom sleeps above a hamburger joint
(The funnel goes up by his bedroom window.)
Day and night the extractor drones and drones.
Dreams are crucial to Palestrom, he needs quiet,
But the noise, spindling and wheedling, shuts them out.

So he decided to set things right:
He climbed onto the roof,
And threw his record player down the funnel.
Beethoven's 'Ode To Joy' played for two whole days.

Then the noise began again.

So he threw his bedding down the funnel:
A fountain of feathers flew up,
Then a flock of hummingbirds
Quiet as the rising sun.

Then the noise began again.

So he threw pancake batter down the funnel:
Pancakes came flying out.
People set tables in the street
And ate all-day breakfasts.
What talk there was!
And the maple syrup never stopped flowing.

Then the noise began again.

So he threw sacks of chestnuts down the funnel:
A tree burst up and spread its leaves.
Old people gathered beneath the tree,
Told stories of all they had done and said,
While children played in the branches.

Then the noise began again.

So he threw bags of cement down the funnel:
A tremendous bridge grew out.

It spanned the entire width of London,
And everyone came out to walk that bridge
To see a London they had so long neglected.

Then the noise began again.

So he threw himself down the funnel:
A mass of dreams flew out.
They hollered and bellowed at one another.
What a noise they made!
More noise than the funnel!

And the noise goes on and on.

PALESTROM PONDERS THE IMPORTANCE
OF MODERN LITERATURE

Palestrom stops at BELL, BOOK, AND RADMALL.
He thinks that any shop with a name like that
Deserves to be walked into.
He sees the books of Pound, Lowry, and Isherwood:

They stand in the window display
- Proper in their first edition jackets -
Protected from the falling dust
By coats of smart plastic.

Palestrom thinks if his name was Book,
He would be a dustman, a crook, a teacher -
Anything but a purveyor of books.
For Palestrom, man is obliged to frustrate his destiny.

Palestrom reads the sign above the window:
MODERN LITERATURE. 80 LONG ACRE.
That's a lot of books, thinks Palestrom,
Particularly, if a long acre is long.

Palestrom thinks of THE STRAND BOOKSTORE:
It has twelve miles of books.
But eighty acres, that's another matter.
Is there really that much Modern Literature?

And he imagines all those books stacked on one acre.
Would they be as tall as the Empire State building?
Thousands of people manage to live on one acre;
How many people live in Modern Literature?

III

ANGER THAT KILLS DOG

Dog lives in Parkdale.
He shuts his door and the police kick it down.
They knuckle his face and want his number:
litter was found on the streetcar and they know it was him.
Dog would like to die. People are always staring at him:
he walks like a penguin, one leg shorter than the other;
his face lopsided; his eyes staring from bleeding rims.
He finds his form in scrawled poems that look through the eye of a donut
shot through by the edge of coffee nerves.
Dog, she was punched in the face,
and thrown down the stairs by her husband,
and kicked in the stomach.
She wakes at night: everywhere she sees the eyes of her aborted child,
and the bruise-coloured light comes in waves,
and almost drowns her.
Dog, only nineteen! Where does she go from here?
Dog is afraid to go home:
his boarding house would go up in one flame.
His roommate is drinking kerosene,
clawing the smothering air with bitten nails:
all night shouting jagged obscenities.
Dog has a mouth swollen like a balloon.
The dentist, ever thoughtful, blows another breath into her pain:
he will not take her until she coughs up $50 for the anaesthetist,
so dog goes home and with a safety pin bleeds the abscess.
Anger blows in the wind, turns the snow to black lumps.
Anger cracks the windows, crawls like cockroaches.
Anger is drank, burning like a bottle of Alpenbitters.
Anger whips, anger smashes, anger rips
like the broken jags of a swallowed headlight.

Dog feels that his heart is slipping:
twice he has thrown himself in front of a subway train.
Psychiatrists tell him to train his will and he'll be better,
but he believes his spirit is ripped like a knifed piece of canvas:
his acrylic virtue, the hypocrisy of a dead soul.
The seasons turn about him, he faces the grave.
Dog once broke into a friend's grocery store:
no weapons, only a mother that was five-days hungry.

There was no room in prison, so they locked him up in Canada's most
    notorious psychiatric ward.
Seized by the police, now he is captured by seizures:
and when he cries for a lost friend, he believes that his illness has struck
    again.
(How do they do it, the psychiatric profession?
They convince people who cry they are mentally ill.)
Dog is a baby, cries, and cries:
her supply of milk has been sold so Daddy can drink.
Mom is all alone, can't stand it any longer.
Television is once again dog's baby sitter:
she rolls on the floor, the Mafia are shooting it out.
Anger is like an injection:
one minute you laugh, the next you cry,
you can't even say a sentence straight
for the thoughts are bouncing in your head like Indian rubber.
Steel-grey, the day is shutting down,
the factory is a pit in the temples, droning and droning.
Anger! Anger! Anger! Dog is exploding.
If dog ever comes together as one,
he would break from his chains,
break from the prison camp of his ghetto
and devour the miserable hand that feeds him starch and crumbs
and a zero-dignity that breaks him on all fours.
Dog lives in Parkdale.
We will fight until we are raised.

JOHN

He got lonely.
He lived at home.
He got more lonely.
One day he bought a knife
and went down to the park.
He hid behind a bush.
The first person that passed by,
he jumped

and tried to stab.

The knife was easily knocked from his hand.

There are lots of lonely people.

This is not a poem about bushes.
You can still walk in parks.

This is about what loneliness
will drive a person to do.

What a solution!

He got two years in Penetang.

Do you know what the guards do for fun?

They wrap a wet towel around a prisoner's neck
and pull it tight
till he crumples to the ground unconscious.

John, flat-footed,
not much more than 5 feet tall,
glasses,
walks like Humpty Dumpty.
I can't even imagine him cutting his meat with a knife.

On second thought, this poem is about bushes.
There isn't one, but hundreds and thousands of people hiding behind
     bushes.

Why are there so many lonely people?

Why are so many who are not lonely
NOT BEFRIENDING those who are lonely?

Bushes could be trees if they weren't burdened with so much loneliness.

DOUG

He called the gutter
his private supermarket.

The objects that he found,
he called INTS

for interesting.

He had a special fascination
for screws.

He mounted them on cardboard
in columns

according to their personality:
the fat man,

the jolly,
the depressed,
the outrageous,
the flamboyant,

the pretty,
the quarrelsome, etc.

An old pen,
he would mount on a pile of books

and pretend
it was a spaceship

that after death
he would sail the galaxies in.

Bottletops,
creased by their opening,

he would hang them from strings -

prehistoric birds
that floated above his bed.

Matches,
he kept in a box,

firewood
for after the holocaust.

The pits of cherries
were planets

he carried around
in his pockets.

An inch-high plastic doll
with a sun bonnet that

dwarfs her

is his future wife
in heaven,

their many arguments
he has already dreamt.

A stone
that has the face of an Egyptian,

he places on

a passage in the bible
to guarantee
the survival of his supermarket.

RAY

It was a government job retraining program
for ex-psychiatric patients:

he would take a bolt in his right hand,
and with his left, twirl on a nut,
then he would place it in a plastic bag,
fold it back, and staple it.

For eight hours a day,
five days a week.

His pay, $1/hr.

Then he would walk seven blocks home
through the 100° afternoon.

His luxury, a shower,

But sometimes the water
did not have the strength
to reach the top floor of the boarding house,
and the sweat hardened on his body
like a thin layer of icing sugar.

Tired, he would return to his room.
He would sit hunched on the edge of his bed
wanting to swing up his legs
and lie back on his pillow.

But he would sit watching the stack of newspapers
that his roommate piled up in the middle of the room,
and he would watch his roommate lying on his bed
flick another burning cigarette

and he would watch it roll towards the newspaper.

Half the table was burnt
from cigarettes ground into the wood.

There was a smoke stain on the ceiling
that looked like a star about to crash,

week after week after week,
until Ray, so afraid,

turned himself into the hospital.

41

LAWRENCE

He had come to Toronto to change his character, or to kill himself.
On the bus ride down he gave half of his money to an old alcoholic who
    said he was broke.

From the beginning he lived on the street.

He ate nothing but bread and jam, and the odd piece of fruit.
Often he thought about his Grandmother who brought him up for his first
    five years and loved jam.
One day he threw his jar of jam into the lake.
He didn't deserve jam!
He should have been dead weeks ago.

With his last money, he bought a loaf of bread from the Harbord Bakery.
It was a French stick with this wonderful articulation of ribs across the
    top.
He hadn't eaten for several days, but it was too beautiful to eat.

With the French stick tucked under his arm, he walked down to City Hall.
Three boys were standing at a drinking fountain.
Without them noticing, he slipped in front of them and started to drink.

They were startled by his presence.
'Heh man, that guy sounds like a horse.'
'Look at that piece of bread, some piece of bread, eh?'

He felt so conspicuous as he walked across the square
that he took off his jacket and wrapped the bread in it.
He was wishing death on the boys, why couldn't they leave him alone?
Then he felt guilty, he started wishing that they had a loaf of bread like
    he did,
that they could know the enjoyment of it.

He sat down on a bench where no one could see him.
After an interminable time, he broke down, decided to have a tiny piece
    of bread,
but when he unwrapped it, half the loaf was gone.

He knew that God had shared it with the boys.

For the next 6 months, he walked 10 miles a day, 1800 miles.
From Kensington Market to Harbord Bakery, Spadina and College
     Street, up to St. Clair, across to Runnymede,
he collected day-old, and older bread that found its way to the back door,

and every evening, he spread out his wares on the steps of the Scott
     Mission:
French sticks, Chelsea buns, rye bread, whole wheat bread, bagels,
     puffed-up loaves of crusty white,
the selection spread itself finer than any baker's display,
and for all those who passed by, it was absolutely free.

WHERE DO BROTHERS COME FROM?

I was out surveying my garden.
Like a deep scratch the sun had cracked the soil;
The string marking off the vegetables drooped;
The little iron fence had fallen;
The tomato plants stood on their lone islands,
Shaking in the warm breeze;
The log in the corner had turned orange.
I bent down to listen to the lettuce
(It had been planted for one long week.)
I heard a voice push up. A leaf appeared.
IT LOOKED LIKE ME. I was shocked. It grew and grew.
I stepped back, drawing to my full height.
He stood there - the same height as me -
But he wasn't me, he was my brother.
Of course, I had no brother, but he stood there.
He had a root-like scar on his forehead.
His eyes were marked by the rivers of the world;
His hands marked by the deserts of five continents.
He asked me about the door leaning against the garage.
I said that it had been there for years,
The grey paint was peeling to green.
With light steps we walked over to the door,
He pulled the handle, we passed through...
It was a road I had never been on.
We walked on the backs of a thousand animals;
Trees had the leaves of a hundred races.
He told me the sky was his friend,
It had passed through his heart innumerable times.
He told me that for weeks on end he had been a house:
The attic room had conversed with the red moon,
But sometimes the top floor plunged to the basement,
And other times the cold and dust of the basement drifted upstairs.
He told me about the three years he'd been a market place
- No meat - only fish, and vegetables, and fruit,
But when he laid the fish in their neat rows,
They had swam back to the sea;
And when he stacked the fruit in their symmetrical piles,
They had flown back to their trees.
And before that, he had been a hill in a park,

But people had littered him with the silver of their gum wrappers,
And the teeth of clouds chewed up his greenness.
What was worse, was night: that was a terrible time for him.
His beard grew roots and pulled his face into the ground:
Dark stars and bright shells circled his eyes.
And we looked at each other, and he told me one more thing:
All he asked for was stillness, and a little love
That shone with one star constant as a blade of grass.

LIFE

I saw her eyes.
I was standing on the wharf.
She threw herself to the sharks.
I screamed till I was sick.

Several days later I met a girl at the dancehall.
She was pregnant.
She had the same look in her eyes.
I asked her to marry me.

She was from New York.
She said she was going home tomorrow, but she'd write me back.
I was hitching just outside of Miami.
They arrested me and threw me in jail, said I should rot.

I don't know how she knew, but a letter arrived next day,

yes

SCHIZOPHRENIA

It is a fact that eight spirits live in us.

Each night, seven leave
and
the remaining spirit
goes out
and
recruits another seven.

The following night,
seven spirits leave
including
the previous night's recruiter,
and
the newly-designated recruiter
brings back seven new spirits.

Like a one-window room
in
steaming hot weather,
circulation
is crucial.

Schizophrenia
is
when the recruiter
stays
an extra night.

He knows you one night better.
He feeds off your confusions,

and stronger,
he stays another night,

and growing pleased with his new habitat,
he asks the other seven to stay,

and they, eager to accept the invitation,

move in with their best video equipment,

and you star
in their continual diet

of horror shows.

DRINA JOUBERT (1944-1985)

Three times three is pain,
and twice infinity is ribs cracked
with no roof over one's head,
scars letting in rain and lightning.
I tramped from hostel to hostel,
mother's ashes loose in my pocket.
Three hours past the freezing of midnight,
knocking on the door of Walpole House,
two faces peered through the peek hole,
said they smelled liquor, go away!
(How do you smell liquor through a closed door?)
I turned back into the cold and snow.

I saw a bed in the snow.
It wanted me to lie down:
I did, and I almost died.

Three times three is pain,
and nine are the days left to live.
From the hospital to a hostel.
Half my side is bitten by cockroaches;
a mouse crawled over my face;
my shoes were stolen. I remembered
how I used to hide under my mother's bed
to listen to her breathing. Now,
there is only the breath of the day,
and what it takes away from me. Sister,
if you would only reach out to me.

I saw a knife in the snow.
It wanted me to grasp it; it wanted me
to thrust it into my chest.

Three times three is pain.
Infinity breaks through my eyes.
Sitting on a bench in Allen Gardens,
I watch the falling snow consume
my footprints. Spring will be soon.
The grass will not be for me;

49

neither the daffodils, nor the crocuses.
Last night I curled up on the floor of an abandoned truck.
The softest black closed around me.
I put out my hand to push it away,
but I was too weak, far too weak.
Two kids found me. They wouldn't even touch me.
They poked me with a stick to see if I was dead.

I saw a chasm in the snow.
Black was the chasm I entered.
Black were the days; black, night; black, death.

PARC CAMPING TRIP

We came to that camp thirty-five of us.
One of us had held up a Mac's Milk at knife point asking for the angel
    of light, and was jailed for two years;
One of us finding a wounded bee on Yonge Street crossed the city with
    the bee in a matchbox and released it in High Park;
One of us could make no sense of Marco Polo and multiplication tables
    and spelling of words he would never use and quit school at 14, and
    they dragged him off to a mental hospital;
One of us always carried a dictionary in his coat pocket, words were the
    substance of his life, he said, words were the colour of his hair, the
    colour of his eyes, the colour of his skin, words were the motion of
    his blood;
One of us, so hungry, had once stolen a can of tuna fish, and crying on
    the curb because he could not open it, had been arrested, and with no
    room in jail, they had locked him away in the most harrowing of
    psychiatric wards;
One of us collected everything he came across - buttons, loose pieces of
    thread, the inner foil of cigarette packages, broken twigs, safety pins,
    elastics: for they were the hearts of the unwanted, and he was their
    saviour;
One of us talked about his dreams and the colour of billboards and a knife
    and the sun ploughing fields of blood, and we were all pulled into his
    misery;
One of us was shunted from one foster home to twenty others, and now
    he tramps back and forth across Canada, never able to stay in one
    place more than a few months;
Many of us have never known our mothers and fathers;
Many of us have seen our mother's face at a door, around a corner, in a
    crowd, across the way, but when we arrived, she was gone,
And even when we finally located her, we were too afraid to announce
    ourselves.

We came to that camp thirty-five of us.
Only one of us had luggage, and that was a garbage bag with a change
    of clothes and a box of water colours;
Most of us had never been out of the city;
Most of us confined to Parkdale,
Confined to boarding houses,
Confined to injections and pills and brief stays in the hospital,
Confined to sitting around and cards and no money,

Confined to coffee and cigarettes and the never ending humiliation of
    having to bum them daily,
Confined to fits and twitching and the restless jerking of bodies,
Confined to nightmares, sweating, dry mouths, and the terrible itching of
    fingers.
None of us had ever been to a camp where there was a lodge and cabins
    with beds and blankets, two fire places, a ping-pong table, on a lake,
    fishing rods, a baseball diamond, walking trails.

We came to that camp thirty-five of us.
The hospital bus, looking every bit like a hospital bus, painted like a
    nurse's uniform, bumped down the highway,
And when it stopped, and backed up, and turned down a dirt road,
    stopping before a lodge, where the lake lapped onto the beach and the
    old dock with its peeling red paint seemed a pathway to the sun,
Someone said, 'This place is too good for us,'
And we sat there in silence, no one moved, what were we to do?
And then the bus turned into mother's old shoe, and the laces flew through
    the eyeholes, and the tongue flopped open,
And we all spilled out:
There was grass to walk in,
There was sand,
There was water,
There were leaves red and yellow clinging to the branches,
There were stairs, and rooms to wander through,
Mattresses to lie down on,
Chairs to pull up around the fire,
And eyes travelled the pathway of the flame
And came to rest on some memory,
And there was the kiss of warmth,
And John who I had never heard speak,
Spoke in enduring length, 'How long are we going to stay here?'

IV

IN MY HOUSE

I carry laughter in my back pocket.
I carry it from room to room because
there are no lightbulbs. At times,
laughter is better than electricity,

then it wilts like an old cherry,
and I'm left with a pit of darkness.
I crawl to the basement, try to find
my old pair of shoes. It's not easy.

Sometimes they are buried beneath the apples,
sometimes in the coal, once or twice
I've found them hanging from the water pipes.
Many times, they're impossible to find.

Still, I try to be patient,
because when I do find them,
I open up their tongues, slip them on
- their laces never the same colour twice -

then I don't need light, I don't need dark,
I can walk up the stairs of my house,
I just glide, and the stairs are transparent,
and the banisters are sunlight, and

the few times I have passed through the roof,
I have been the sky and light, and all
the misery and happiness that humans endure.
For a moment, I have felt totally alive.

AUNT ALLISON'S BUNKHOUSE

seconds later I collapsed to the floor

I felt my legs separate from my body
and float to the ceiling

they picked me up and carried me
to another room, dumped
me on a bunk bed

when I awoke next morning, no one
was stirring

I lay there helplessly, saw on the floor
a newborn kitten

squashed

his guts squirting out his mouth

I wanted to touch it, prove
it was real

two guys walked into the room
with a shovel, scooped up
the kitten

I heard them say
a litter had been born last night
under my bed

the toilet flushed

every part of my body s.c.r.e.a.m.e.d
o.u.t.

WRITTEN ON KLEENEX

My mother has one arm. It is artificial.
My father would invite friends over to watch her
hold boiling pots without pot holders.
When I was young, we had a dog called Tobacco.
When we ran out of cigarettes, we would shave him.
My worst dream is when square-jawed men and women
huddle around my ice-cream head, and take two scoops from my
    forehead.
Sometimes they place a birthday candle in each scoop,
then blow them out.
I am sure that the stars are kerosene,
that they have a limited life.
How would you like my job sweeping out parking lots
for pennies?
I spend my years collecting discarded cards.
I have never found the two of hearts.
When people take an interest in me,
I know their heart has been blown out their back, and
they are on the verge of attacking me with bayonets.
Every time I open a door, my hand sticks.
The circle I was born in neither opens, nor closes.
It just withers up, terrorized by a world of impenetrable eyes.
When I look in the mirror, I see a map of Japan where
the wolf has his paws cut off,
and the bloody stumps are stuck in white sugar.
Maybe in 300 years you might wipe the tears from your eyes...
but I can't wait that long!

H.

Tired, I think about kleenex thrown into a toilet bowl of very yellow piss.

In a fit, I smashed my glasses beneath the screeching streetcar.
I paid the driver two tokens for doing me a favour.

I got in a fight with a lady's face that was pancake white.

I understand people who wear earrings through their nose.

I hate it when my tortured head is diagnosed as migraines.
That's something birds do. I don't have birds across my forehead.

Why do children like letting mud ooze up between their toes?
Don't ask me; my shoes are black beans.

When people look at my hands, they turn away.

Sometimes I see my ribs like the unfinished hull of a ship.
They float out across the sea and sink.

My day is like a century.
When I lie down, a hot breath breathes down my neck.

Birds eat more than I do.
Their nest is a thread of silk compared to my coffin.

I should be friends with the worms.

TWO PAIRS OF SHOES

Yesterday I read a poem by Kenneth Patchen
about an old pair of shoes that he saved
and placed on the closet shelf to remember
his years of tramping the streets to find a job;
the nail that dug into his heel always reminding
him of the recession; the scar on the toe-cap
from a policeman's horse charging the so-called mob;
the right shoelace longer than the left, in memory
of William Blake; how his wife called those shoes
boats that sailed to the eternal heavens
and always brought him back to her. In the poem,
Patchen was thinking how twenty years later,
he had all the things he wanted in earlier years:
rent paid to the end of the month, records, books,
tailor-made cigarettes, but if he had the choice,
every time he would choose the life of those shoes.

Some months ago, I was in a Roots store
and I overheard the salesman recommending
a pair of shoes to a customer. He said
that he owned a pair and had had them for 6 weeks,
and still there wasn't a single water mark on them.
It was mid-winter, and I wondered how he did it.
I imagined him walking barefoot through the snow
with his shoes tightly clutched in his hands,
and soon as he entered a doorway, he would put on his shoes.
But then he put an end to my surmising, he said he rarely went outside:
weren't underground concourses such a marvellous invention?
And I thought of him saving his shoes:
perfect, heels unworn, stitches intact, leather uncreased.
What memories would he have? fabulous adventures
midst the alligator belts? love relations with the lights
warming the avocados? stationary ecstacies at Grand and Toy?
secret provocations behind the silk scarves?
In twenty years time he would probably look back at those years
as a troublesome time when he still had to walk.

MICE

Once mice ran in the fields -
vision in our green lives.

Then, when we built houses
that swallowed up the fields,
mice lived in the walls.

We fed them spilt coffee
and cake crumbs and jam
sandwiches. Our carelessness
was their party.

Then a few people,
with nerves like lightning
rods, had a vision
of God's face hovering
tenderly over
a mouse.

After that, mice
never came out
from their holes.

They fed off the
spirit in the walls.
And cockroaches,
like untended herds
of cattle,
fed on our
crumbs.

I hear the mice at
night, like the blood
that runs through
my body, but

I wish I could have
one last glimpse.
The world has gotten
so much harder.

Some say it's a battle zone.
What I see most is
the interminable scurry
of cockroaches.

I wish the mice
would return.

SPIDER LOVE

He lay on his back, his
head resting on a lumpy
pillow, the hospital sheet
pulled up to his neck.

A spider hung several inches above his face.

From the ceiling, it would lower
itself on a silvery thread,
talk to him for hours.
And, when the man grew cold,
it would spin a web
over his face, keeping him warm.

When she came in, the spider
would return to the ceiling.

One day, she proclaimed she
had crushed the spider.
He said, No, I still
see him on the ceiling;
he's resting on the seventh circle.

Oh your damn spider, she said,
I pinched him between my fingernails
like a common wood lice.
He said, Impossible, he
talks to me like water.

She said, I crushed him beneath
my heel. He said, My spider
never goes that low.

She said, I laughed when
he wriggled beneath my
burning cigarette. He
said, My spider is
a spark in the night.

That night the man grew
cold. The spider
came down, spun its web.
Later, she swept in,
held his hand as
the last remnants
of warmth ran
from his body.

COCOON II

Harold, 80,
told me this story:

his mother, 101,
resides
in
an old-age home

and
one night

she
with
her friends
Elsie, 103,
Ruth, 105,
and the youngster
of the group,
Betty, 99,

were watching
the Thursday night
movie

'Cocoon.'

They weren't actually being
rejuvenated,

but they were enjoying
it,

and then the old bag
on duty
crossed the room
in
a flurry of starch
and turned off
the TV
at precisely 9 o'clock,

snapping,
'Okay ladies, bedtime!'

And when they protested,
she brusquely
said,
'You'll have another
chance
to see it,'

and herded
them off.

LAST DAYS

Those were the days
we wandered through shopping malls,
we nuzzled up to stuffed panda bears
and tied alligator belts around our waist.

Those were the days
our tongues dipped into scoops of Hagen Daz,
we gulped down cinnamon buns from Kansas,
adroitly flicked pistachio shells into ashtrays.

We praised the ingenuity of architects
for palm trees that grew up through the tiled floors,
we submitted ourselves to the wandering chiropractors
who every Sunday preached the gospel of good posture.

Those were the days
we hung wicker baskets from our arms,
filled them with sausages hanging from the ceiling of Spritzels,
tried on Birkenstocks to feel the soothing fingers of sales girls.

Those were the days
we filched quarters from the water fountains,
scribbled closing down prices on windows,
fashioned canes out of coat hangers for the walk to our cars.

Once in a while we stood in the sun,
but we missed our shopping malls,
we missed the flurry of busy hands and wrapping paper,
we missed the aroma of air conditioning,

we missed the subtle humming of Nieman Marcus,
we missed the proliferation of designer shopping bags,
we missed the delicacy of lovers kissing on escalators,
we missed the immaculate creases of La Ferrara suits.

Those were the days,
we wore diamond rings to remember extinquished stars,
we praised the reliability of our 14-karat watches,
and a revolution in retailing burnt a path to our every desire.

Those were the days
we exploded bottles of Panthere de Cartier to drown out the smell of
    hotdog stands,
we brought to the attention of managers dirty specks on skylights,
we feigned collapse on exquisite beds of Notari linen.

Those were the days
we ate candy floss for afternoon zest,
talked to mannikins when the going was bad,
wore flamboyant colours so children would notice.

We went to Ruby Tuesdays for Ellery Queens,
slapped warning stickers across signs that advertized everyday values,
filled out application forms to win Atari computers,
name: beyond computation; address: half-way to heaven.

Those were the days:
and even if we had to be down on hands and knees,
scrubbing every square inch of shopping mall floor,
we would rather be there...

AD FOR THE FUTURE

In 1953
after a series of nuclear explosions
in Utah,
sheepherders claimed
that an abnormal number
of ewes and lambs
were dying.
Of course,
the Atomic Energy Commission
denied
any responsibility for the deaths.
However, one official
admitted
the easiest thing to do
would be to pay
for these sheep,
but if they paid,
every woman
that got pregnant
and every woman that didn't
would sue.
(Exact words.)
Later, the AEC
followed up with a study
which claimed
that in subsequent lambing seasons
there was a significant
reduction in birth weights
which meant
the lambs were born dead,
or died within a few days.
Finally, in a fit
of benevolence,
the AEC announced
that it might provide the sheepherders
with a small sum of money
in the form of a
'desert range nutrition research project,'
the only strings being

that the project could not research
radiation issues.

When the war breaks out,
most of the world will be
extinquished.
5 people will survive.
4 of them will be government,
and the fifth
much to their chagrin
will be a reasonably
intelligent person.
The four will launch
a public relations campaign
to convince the one
that the war
was an unfortunate mishap,
and happily
it was contained
because of the wise precautions
undertaken by the government.
And to demonstrate
their commitment to the future,
they will wrangle a deal
to finance
'the world repopulation research project,'
and although the one
belabours the fact
that no women have survived,
the four
will stipulate
that the condition once-called pregnancy
be excluded
from the study.

DAY OF SEVEN SUNS

When I return to the house of seven suns,
there will be no man with his pistol at the doorstep,
drunk, and aiming at the sun,
swearing he will shoot six of them from the sky.
No, there will be the faint smell of sunflowers,
and the moon will lead a path through the doorway,
and inside the emperor will be stitching a rip in his shirt.
I'll stand at the doorway, watch the needle dip and soar,
watch as the emperor turns bronze in the silver light.
He will stop sewing, and I will go over to him:
I will tell him about my years in the garish-lighted city,
where I saw men bent over searching for rat holes,
and when they found one they would shrivel up
and climb down it for a lifetime of work.
Wives would stand at the top of these holes and shout down words of
     encouragement
till hearts filled with the dust of distance.
And when the leaves turned dry and crackly,
husbands would write messages to their wives,
but they were lost in TV screens, perfume, and voyages to shopping
     malls.
And I also came across people who rejected these rat holes,
but they cowered in their room blinded by the sky of seven suns.
One I met said, whenever he went out,
seven men the colour of blue storms would spring up from the pavement,
and he thought, one for each day of the week
- and where did he belong? -
but they compelled him to follow.
They pulled coins from their pockets, sucked them like candy.
They laughed a hideously thin laugh.
Invariably they would lead him to a whale-grey house
that was the body of his dead girlfriend
with windows as fleshy as blood blisters.

And the emperor waved his hand, and I was quiet.
He told me that last night he had slept in the sleep of the Monster Tsun
- that half-dog, half-tiger -
who sitting on his haunches had cradled the emperor in his arms,
holding him to his chest, not breathing one breath the entire night.

And birds nesting in his pointed ears slept the sleep of unheard of skies,
and mice burrowed in the fur of his shoulders slept the sleep of unseen
    stars,
and the emperor tucked under his chin slept the sleep of seven suns.

And he had a dream:
he came to a wall with holes eaten out by the sun,
he flowed through the holes, gushed out the other side.
He flowed down the Yellow River, the Ganges, the Nile, the Hudson.
He met peoples who made no weapons, and held councils of music.
He met peoples who lived in the street and fed on dust,
and row after row of them died in the gutters.
He met peoples who lived in mud huts, conversed with ancestors in the
    trees,
and chased antelope on foot through the blue air of days and hills.
He met peoples who held mirrors in their eyes and spoke the same words,
who stored their minds in deposit boxes, and grew missiles as tall as
    forests.
'And in my dream,' he said, 'I was overcome by weariness,
I could neither praise, nor condemn,
but then I came to the end of rivers that met in a cloud of air.
I breathed for once, breathed and breathed
an aura where all the great men and women had walked
and, for one moment, they all came together in me,
and the death of children, torture, war, hatred, greed,
I knew I must fight against them till the end of life.
And the Monster Tsun faded above me
- his shaggy, bearded face converged into a narrow spot of light -
and I walked through the streets exclaiming,
''My people, my people, my people,
I have fed, feed from me.'''

FEET ARE NOT WINGS

I have written several books about my feet.
They have never been best sellers.

Once at the stag party of a friend, a stripper was hired, and when the groom lined up for her services, three of us hurled empty beer bottles into the fireplace. One of us got into a fight with the groom, and after we had pulled them apart rolling in the glass, the three of us tore off our clothes and ran naked down to Yonge Street. Next morning, the police followed our bloody footprints in the snow.

I don't want to talk about past episodes of my feet.
I want to talk about the present.

Last night was another night of feet. Again, they were bare. I had to go into the basement. The steps are very steep, and worn in the centre as if hundreds of feet had tread on them. I can understand steps up to the bedroom being worn, but not steps to the basement. I took my first step. A rusty nail ripped into my heel, tearing out a large hunk of skin. At first there was no bleeding, but I could feel the blood welling up. Then it burst. I went upstairs and soaked my heel in a bowl of milk. Slowly, petals of blood rose to the surface like lily pads, and spread out till white was blotted out completely. I then wrapped a leaf around my heel and bound my foot with golden hair.

(I thought of her; wanting her. I'd met her several week before the stag. When I told her about the stag, we were outside. The snow was melting. She stepped off the kerb into a backed-up sewer, sat down, and started to splash water over herself. Brown-coloured drops hung in her golden hair. I was terrified. And how I loved her.)

My foot felt lighter. The lightness ascended to my knee. I could see my leg being amputated. When I'm worried, I always do the same thing. I pick up the nearest book and try to lose myself in it. This time it was an anthology of postwar Polish poetry. The first poem I read was about a group of farmers who watched HAMLET beneath an apple tree, and when they were full of despair, they went home and, falling to the floor, kissed the feet of their wives.

I have not watched HAMLET for years; I rarely think about HAMLET, but still I want to fall to the floor, kiss her feet. And this is what the poem omitted: I wish she'd fall to the floor and kiss my feet. I don't want her to be subservient to me, or me to her, but we are so busy with our little ambitions, we have failed to notice our separate flights. Feet are not wings. When they stop running, they dig into the earth like roots.

FATE

I lived at No. 9

you lived at No. 11

a Chinese family lived at No. 13
the grandfather died from cancer
the oldest son broke his arm
the daughter failed her year at school

they went to the soothsayer

she told them to change their street number

after they had gone from door to door with a petition
the house I lived in became No. 7
yours No. 9
the Chinese family's No. 11

you had lived next door for 8 months
and never once had I seen you
till you came to the door with my mail

Cronyn you said

yes

and we joked about soothsayers
and you stayed for 3 days

and in 3 years we had 3 children

I will always believe in soothsayers

TALE OF TWO ELASTICS (1)

found an elastic band on a cobbled street
of Amsterdam.
a white elastic.
Wendy was five-months pregnant
waiting for the results from amniocentesis.
nerves!
what would our decision be?
every life is sacred.

kept the elastic. was sure
it was lucky.
kept it in my coat pocket till
we received the results -
everything's fine.
kept it in my coat pocket
for the birth.

miraculous birth at home.
Chloe!

kept the elastic. many
times my fingers
played with it,
stretched it,
scrunched it in a
ball.

not so white any longer.
thought of washing it.
started to tear in places.

feared it would snap.

feared I would lose it.
how many times pulling out
my gloves,
it fell to the
ground.

everyday, more and more afraid of
losing it.
Wendy said, put it in a
drawer.
after two years, hung it
around the neck
of a bottle on top
of my speaker,
beneath the shade of
my lamp.

forgot about it. weeks later
looked.
looked again. saw
no elastic.
the elastic

had melted -

a straggly
necklace
bonded to the
glass.

at first, thought it
was a
sign
of bad luck.

then tried to
convince myself:
good luck.

puzzled over
the symbolism.
was it a
warning?

parents wear children
like a burden
around
their neck.

no!

I'll wear my
children like
a holiday.

BABY SLICK

A mother holds her baby
on her hip.
She sways back and forth
looking out at the ocean.

The wind, the waves, the salt
blow towards them.
The slender leaf of a palm tree
almost touches her shoulder.

Below them, the beach.
Coke tins. Globs of oil. Fat bodies.
Through the eyes of the baby,
a sail, a cloud, a white cap.

The baby is laughing.

The mother ruffles his hair.

NEW TIMES

I was sitting
at the kitchen
table

with
one hand out

to pacify
Chloe my 18-
month-old
daughter

determined
to read
an article
on

nightclubbing
in
London

and she
kept plopping
one object
after
another

into
my hand.

I read
about

blitz kids -
a hedonistic
hybrid
of punk
outrage

with New
Romantic
dress sensibility

that in a pre-
Aids era
clubbers
saw
themselves
as creators
rather
than consumers
now they
are
more detached

VOYEURS

while I sit
there
holding
in
my hand

three onions
and
one potato.

TALE OF TWO ELASTICS (2)

difficulty in conceiving, found another
elastic, tan-coloured, one
of those omnipresent
elastics that litter hallways
and sidewalks, that once
bound a packet of
Her Majesty's Royal
Mail.

this time, felt arbitrary. can
you repeat something
once spontaneous?

tied it to my key ring. how
many times it untied itself,
fell to the sidewalk.
Wendy said, give it up.
it's not the same thing.
maybe it's preventing
conception.

five months later, Wendy pregnant.

two months into the pregnancy,
fingering my keys, elastic
snapped.
made a great effort to downplay it,
relied elastic, but
as I pulled it tight,
snapped again.
held two pieces in my hand.
couldn't throw them out.
dropped them in the bottle
on top of my speaker.

next day, Wendy gushed
blood. was sure she'd miscarried.
on the way to the hospital,
staring through a rain-splashed window,

my eyes fixed on the roof of a
house under construction -
a blanket was rolled up
like swaddling clothes.
cruel. even the rooftops
shout what we've lost.

at the hospital, Wendy taken off
for tests. hours later,
a nurse led me down a maze of
halls. Wendy on a bed
with sheets pulled up to
her neck. was sure she'd
had a D and C - painful
scraping out - elastic
snapped.

Wendy sat up, slight smile, held out
a darkened plate, like an x-ray.
what do you see? she said.
looks like a cabbage roll
with a thing in it.
and what's there? she said, pointing.
oh ya, another thing.
they're alive.
you mean...
yes, and she's laughing, yes,
TWINS.

BREATHING WITH GRANDAD

I was sitting in the corner
with Koy nestled in the crook of my arm,
rocking back and forth.
I could be a mother, I thought.
This is so peaceful.

Two nurses talked about a 2 lb. baby,
and how cute he was.
(Ten years ago he would never have lived.)
A man, peering into the incubator of his child,
chanted a passage from the Koran.
Koy, for the first time, had been detached from the intravenous tubes.
The doctor said he was 'safe' now.
I attributed it to the rubber giraffe
someone had placed in his incubator.

I looked down.
A fine thread of burning
shot from my chest to my stomach.
Koy had stopped breathing.

I pulled at his chin,
rubbed his chest.
Was I imagining things?
I remembered a doctor saying, 'Babies simply forget how to breathe.'
I began to shout, Breathe! Breathe!

Solid breaths,
in-out,
in-out,
I had never been so aware of my breathing,
in-out.

And then I felt another breath join mine,
in-out,
two breaths joined together,
swelling out till they filled the room,
the room was our breathing,
our breathing was the room,

the room housed us,
we were the stairs that climbed
to the attic, and through the relics of family history,
that climbed through the roof,
stairs that made their way to you.

He's named after you.
We knew how you hated your name,
so we lifted Koy from the middle - Verschoyle.
Tonight we breathed with you.

MY BOOKCASE IS A BABY WHALE
WITH 3000 TIGERS

For sixteen years I had my own room, a half-room, wide as I am tall, and
maybe twice that length.
It was filled with books and records, two desks, a slew of art posters, and
an old IBM typewriter.

A month ago I gave up my room to share with my four-year-old daughter,
Chloe.
I still have a desk in the corner, and, along one of the walls, from one end
to the other, stacked to the ceiling, orange crates filled with books.
Along the other wall, her bunk bed.

Chloe and I are sitting on the top bunk. We are reading Kenneth Lilly's
ANIMALS.
We read that there are less than 3000 tigers left in the world.
I try to explain how few tigers that is; there's that many people living
within a few blocks of us. And there's only that many tigers in the whole
world!
She says, as many tigers as your books?
Yes, I laugh, each book is a tiger.

Then we read about the sperm whale; how the new-born are one of the
world's largest babies, four metres long.
I tell Chloe that's about the length of my bookcase.
She says, your bookcase is a baby whale with 3000 tigers in its stomach.

Why didn't I give up my room earlier?

ACKNOWLEDGEMENTS

ENGLAND

AMBIT: Dream Room, Palestrom Wants to Be a Toilet, Palestrom Unloved, Palestrom Trains His Body to Break Out in Thorns, Palestrom Reverses the Fall of the Rain, Palestrom Feels Good, Doug, Schizophrenia
THE ECHO ROOM: Ray, Cocoon II
IRON: I Want to Bake My Brain in a Birthday Cake, To Apollinaire, H., Feet Are Not Wings
JOE SOAP'S CANOE: Lawrence
SLOW DANCER: Palestrom Plays at House, Palestrom Is a Dream of Noise, PARC Camping Trip, Two Pairs of Shoes, Spider Love, Last Days, Baby Slick, My Bookcase Is a Baby Whale with 3000 Tigers
SCRATCH: Mice
STRANGE MATHEMATICS: Nickelodeon
TUBA: Wardrobe Upbringing
THE WIDE SKIRT: Life, In My House, Aunt Allison's Bunkhouse, Written on Kleenex
ZENOS: The Day Has Dirty Hair

THE CREAM OF THE TROUBADOUR COFFEE HOUSE (ANTHOLOGY): I Want to Bake My Brain in a Birthday Cake, Where Do Brothers Come From? Drina Joubert, PARC Camping Trip

CANADA

THE CUCKOO'S NEST: Anger that Kills Dog, Where Do Brothers Come From? PARC Camping Trip
THE FIDDLEHEAD: Drina Joubert
WAVES: John

UNITED STATES

KAYAK: Blue Begonias, Dream Room, The Discarded Glove
NEW DIRECTIONS: Dream Room, Palestrom Wants to Be a Toilet, Palestrom Unloved, Palestrom Trains His Body to Break into Thorns, Palestrom Reverses the Fall of the Rain, Palestrom Feels Good

*   *   *